Table of Contents

TWO ON THE AISLE, PLEASE

What fun it was for me to take a break from my piano arranging of hymns and gospel songs to do this collection of Lerner & Loewe favorites...actually, *my* favorites of Alan Jay Lerner and Frederick Loewe. Their gift of words and music is inspiring to me, and just for the record, I have committed to memory all of the lyrics to "My Fair Lady" (including Henry Higgins *and* Eliza Doolittle's parts). I found in their writings excellent opportunity to use the rich harmonies and bright rhythmic patterns I love to play, and love to write out so others can play them too. (Please play them carefully, observing these very important sharps and flats which have been placed there with great care!)

"Thank Heaven for Little Girls," page 2; "I Talk to the Trees," page 4; "If Ever I Would Leave You," page 15; and "Gigi," page 27; are my very favorites. Though, now that I mention it, "Get Me to the Church on Time," on page 18 is pretty good, too. And so is "Camelot" on page 12. I guess I'm just too close to be objective; kind of like asking me which of my children is the cutest!

But here's one thing I know for certain, a great cry will arise from pianists throughout the land when they get to my setting in the key of F# on page 30. For some reason, since the beginning of time, pianists have avoided sharp keys. Does anyone know *why*? If you take this as a challenge to master the F# tonality, you will certainly dazzle your piano-playing friends when you can whip off "They Call the Wind Maria" in the key of F *AND* F#! (After that, any Chopin Etude will seem like child's play!)

The houselights are beginning to dim, so you'd better get to the piano and play through these pieces for us. My wife and I have great seats, orchestra level, middle section, two on the aisle. Play well.

Los Angeles, California, 1980 — FRED BOCK

Gentry Publications

Thank Heaven for Little Girls

ALAN JAY LERNER
(Lyrics not included)

FREDERICK LOEWE
Arranged by Fred Bock

ten.
ten.
mp
15ma
pp

I Talk to the Trees

ALAN JAY LERNER
(Lyrics not included)

FREDERICK LOEWE
Arranged by Fred Bock

8va
15ma
loco
mf
ff
l.h.
r.h.
8va
Lightly
mp
f

ff
ten.
ten.
l.h.
r.h.
8va
mf
8va
15ma

mf
ten.
3
8va
15ma
r.h.
l.h.
8va
3
3
3
8va
ten.
p
3

The Rain in Spain

ALAN JAY LERNER
(Lyrics not included)

FREDERICK LOEWE
Arranged by Fred Bock

Moderato (Habañera tempo)

f
faster
f

3
3
15ma
f
ff
8va

Camelot

ALAN JAY LERNER
(Lyrics not included)

FREDERICK LOEWE
Arranged by Fred Bock

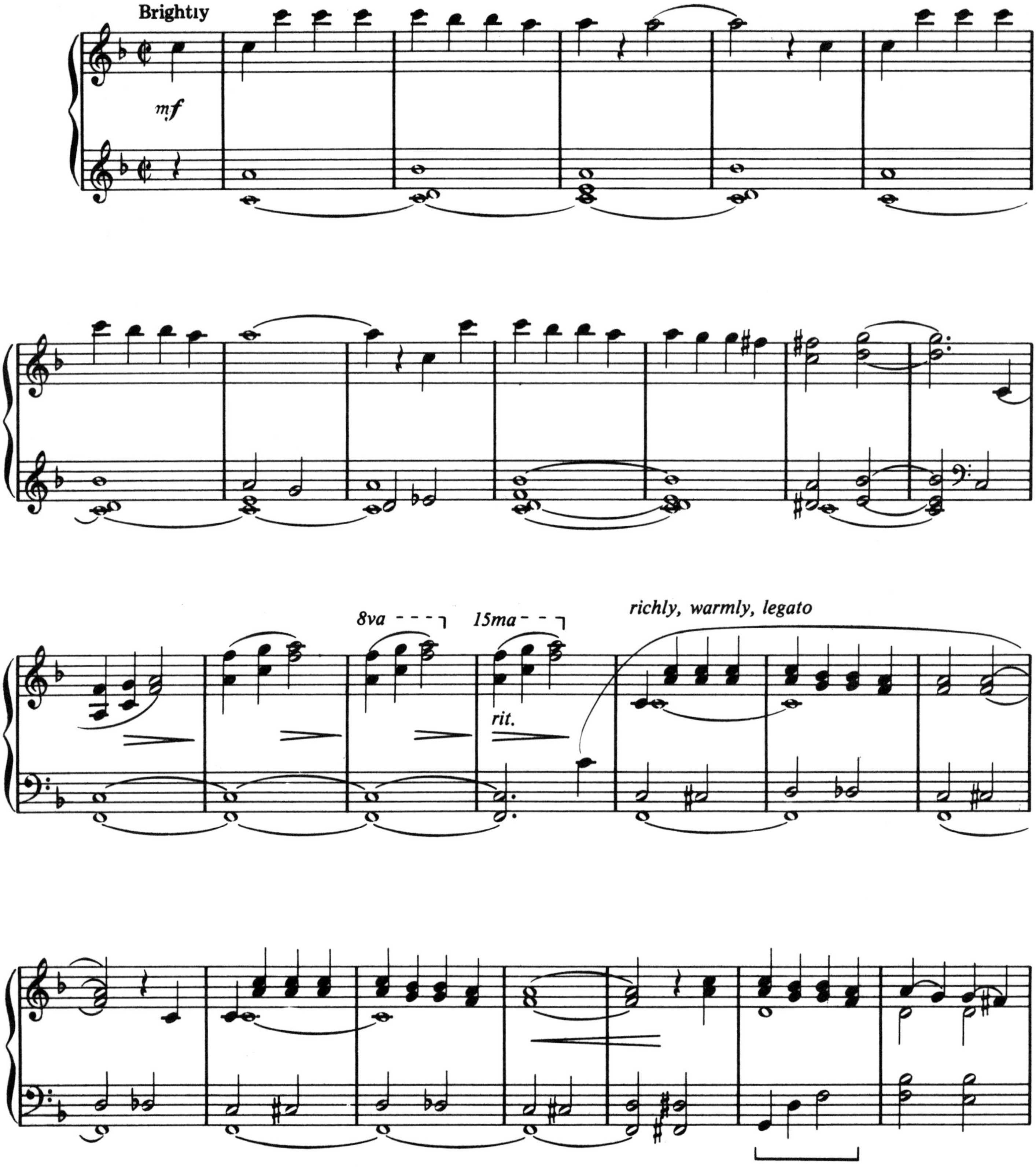

very slowly
8va
rit.
ten.
a tempo
mp
3
4
5
4
8va
8va

a little slower and warmer
ad lib.
mf
f
mp
p
8va

If Ever I Would Leave You

ALAN JAY LERNER
(Lyrics not included)

FREDERICK LOEWE
Arranged by Fred Bock

8va
f
mp
3
r.h.
l.h.
f
mp

broaden
ten. ten.
ten.
8va
r.h.
l.h.
r.h. mf
l.h.

Get Me to the Church on Time

ALAN JAY LERNER
(Lyrics not included)

FREDERICK LOEWE
Arranged by Fred Bock

mp
mf
mp
mf
8va
slowly (like a music box)
mp
8va
a tempo
ff
mf
mp
mf
mp

1.
2.
f
8va
ff
sempre ff

I Could Have Danced All Night

ALAN JAY LERNER
(Lyrics not included)

FREDERICK LOEWE
Arranged by Fred Bock

sim.
smoothly

f
mp
mf
1.
2.
slowing down
slowing even more
ten.
p
r.h.
8va
pp

On the Street Where You Live

ALAN JAY LERNER
(Lyrics not included)

FREDERICK LOEWE
Arranged by Fred Bock

faster
mf

3
ten.
a tempo
mf
ten.
broaden
15ma
f
ff
r.h.
l.h.
ff
8

Gigi

ALAN JAY LERNER
(Lyrics not included)

FREDERICK LOEWE
Arranged by Fred Bock

f
8va
ten.
loco
f
strongly
mf
ten.
ten.
rit.

a tempo
f
ten.
ten.
ten.
ten.
8va
8va
8va
p
mp
ten.
p
ten.

They Call the Wind Maria

ALAN JAY LERNER
(Lyrics not included)

FREDERICK LOEWE
Arranged by Fred Bock

a tempo
f
f

f
a tempo
suddenly much slower and softer
ten.
15ma
l.h.
l.h.
8va
l.h.
8va
mp
r.h.
r.h.
r.h.
r.h.
ff
ten.
black note gliss. downward
l.h.
8va